Kenny Rogers'
AMERICA

Kenny Rogers'
AMERICA

by Kenny Rogers

Foreword by Yousuf Karsh

LITTLE, BROWN AND COMPANY
BOSTON, TORONTO

Library of Congress Cataloging-in-Publication Data

Rogers, Kenny.
    Kenny Rogers' America.
    1. United States—Description and travel—
1981–   —Views.   I. Title.
E169.04.R64   1986   779'.99173   86-10368
ISBN 0-316-75419-6

HAL

DESIGNED BY JEANNE ABBOUD

*Published simultaneously in Canada
by Little, Brown & Company (Canada) Limited*

PRINTED IN THE UNITED STATES OF AMERICA

I dedicate this book to my wife, Marianne, who not only allowed me the time but encouraged me to do this book — I love her . . .

ACKNOWLEDGMENTS

There are many people who have helped to make this work possible.

Special thanks first to John Sexton for giving me *all* the knowledge I have to this date about landscape photography, and also for the beautiful printing job he did. As this books unfolds, you'll see how truly important he's been to me. His friendship and support were and are essential.

Special thanks then to Rob Pincus. Behind every great photographer is a guy carrying equipment. Rob has been Sherpa, friend, ego builder, baby-sitter, film loader and developer, driver, and, more important, an assistant who learned right alongside me and maybe better. Rob, this book is as much yours as mine.

I also want to thank:

Kelly Junkermann, for his photographic assistance as well as his friendship throughout this project;

Bob Shanebrook at Kodak for all his special help and accepting my late-night panicky phone calls for supplies;

Kodak, for a more than generous supply of materials since all pictures were shot with Kodak Tri-X or Tech-pan, developed with HC-110 or Technidal, and printed on Kodak Elite Fine-Art Paper;

Polaroid — all exposures were checked, rechecked, and checked again on Polaroid film;

Norma Smith at Samy's Camera in Los Angeles;

Richard Pine, my agent, for starting me at the top and believing that I could do it.

Special thanks and gratitude are due to Little, Brown and Company for making this opportunity available to me. Most important, my thanks to Fredrica S. Friedman. I can't say enough how encouraging and truly supportive she has been from day one. She was always there as an editor and friend to give me the confidence I needed.

FOREWORD

I saw Kenny Rogers the performer before I met Kenny Rogers the man. On a hot August evening, in Ottawa, I watched this consummate entertainer establish immediate rapport with his audience of thousands. With the enthusiastic fans in the front rows he began a bantering dialogue, at once informal and personal. Even those sitting farther back felt his warmth and reality.

No stranger to footlight magic, I wondered what my reaction would be the next day, when we were to meet in my studio for the first time, away from the mesmerizing concert atmosphere. The handsome man, in casual attire, who bounded into my studio created the same energy and appeal I had witnessed the evening before. We were to share his portfolio of photographs taken in the free time during his crisscrossing of America on concert tours. As we viewed his photographs together, it became increasingly apparent that here was more than the enthusiasm of the casual amateur. Subsequent meetings confirmed that, indeed, the mastery of photography was an all-consuming passion. In contrast to the dynamic interaction with his audience, photography was a creative refuge, something he could do all alone. Behind the camera he must rely on himself only and the considerable creative resources he can bring to bear.

We looked over many of the fine photographs that eventually found their way into this, his first book. His approach — the way he works — is as straightforward as the man himself. I was struck by how quickly he incorporated comments and suggestions to augment his original conceptions. The master of his own entertainment métier, he became the willing open-minded adventurer in a field he was eagerly exploring.

Kenny Rogers has discovered in photography not only a challenging discipline, a keener perception of the unexpected beauty of everyday life, and a new regard for the nuance — in a landscape, in a face — that can easily be missed. He has also discovered the majesty of America.

Yousuf Karsh

Kenny Rogers'
AMERICA

INTRODUCTION

From the dramatic skylines of its great cities to the serene vistas and overpowering landscapes that are part of its natural heritage, America is a diverse, even mysterious, country. Over the past year, I have crisscrossed this land many times. Along the way, I have found what seems to be an inexhaustible treasury of visual riches. Both in the stillness of places far removed from urban life, and in the bustling centers of America's great cities, I have photographed some of this country's most alluring and intriguing physical assets. In the process of shooting this book, I have come to know an America whose inhabitants have many faces, whose cities stimulate the eye in countless ways, and whose varied landscapes create many moods and rhythms. Doing this project has been one of the most rewarding experiences in my life. It has brought me in closer contact with the skylines and vistas of this country's great urban and rural landscapes. And, perhaps even more important, it has opened up a whole new way of seeing the world around me.

The slanting rays of the evening sun on a natural landscape can make it glow with all the magic of a musical phrase. I have seen this quality in the russet-colored badlands of Zion National Park, where sculpted sandstone canyons stretch for miles across the Utah desert. In California, I have climbed the High Sierra to see the mirrorlike stillness of alpine lakes that look like hammocks between granite peaks. I have also seen nature's tranquil beauty in the shadows of a New Mexico sand dune and in the sunlight coming through a willow tree along a Michigan highway. Although the richness of the American landscape is unsurpassed, its cities have their own visual magnetism. From the top of San Francisco's Nob Hill, I have seen the early morning sun through banks of dense fog settled at the base of the Golden Gate Bridge. In Chicago, I have watched railroad tracks trail off into the horizon. And in New York, I have marveled at the diversity of human faces and the drama of huge skyscrapers piercing the blue sky.

I have been on the road for twenty-two years, longer than most performers in this country. I live a hectic, fast-paced schedule that brings me in contact with more than two million people each year, many of whom take pictures of me with their own cameras. With a staff of more than fifty people, including musicians, sound

3

technicians, and road managers, in the course of a year I perform more than a hundred and fifty concerts in a hundred and twenty cities from coast to coast. Whether I am flying my own plane from Los Angeles to Las Vegas, busing from Portland, Oregon, to Tacoma, Washington, or driving a Jeep over rough roads in the Nevada high desert, I have an unparalleled opportunity to see America from the air, land, and sea.

Over the past year, I have discovered there is a strong, though not always clear, relationship between my music and my photography. I think that no artist — a musician, a photographer, a painter — can fence off his living from his creating. The two usually go hand in hand. Even though I try to see my photography as separate from my music, I feel these two disciplines share some specific elements. Both art forms provide a medium — one is visual and one is verbal — for communicating deep feelings and perceptions about the world. Light traveling through space is to photography what the beat is to music — its primary pulse and driving force. Like a moving song, a beautiful photograph travels directly, although silently, to the heart and mind of its viewer, joining the past and present into a powerful image. At its best, a photograph can elevate the spirit, capture the imagination, and transport us, if only for a moment, to a better place.

My interest in photography began more than twenty years ago. My oldest son, Kenny II, had just been born and I was performing with a group called the Bobby Doyle Three. We spent a lot of time on the road playing with the Kirby Stone Four, a well-known jazz group in the early 1960s. One fall, I was relaxing in New Jersey with Kirby Stone. It was one of those crisp, clear days in which the reds and bright yellows of autumn leaves were so spectacular I decided to take some snapshots of my son.

Kirby had an Argus C-3, one of those funky, offbeat cameras with collapsible lens, adjustable f-stop, and speed control. At the time, I was using a Brownie Hawkeye, a bottom-of-the-totem-pole snapshooter. Kirby said, "Kenny, why don't you use the Argus? It will do

a better job." I said, "I have no idea how to use this thing." He put the camera in my hand and explained, "You just put it on 1/125 second at f/8 and shoot. It's that simple." And it was. But the results were not: I got some of the most incredible color photographs I had ever taken. Each leaf was perfect and the colors, from the glow on my son's face to the deep blue sky, had range and depth. Shooting with the Argus made me realize how nice it would be to have a permanent reminder of special moments, not only in my personal life, but in the lives of other people who are important to me.

At the time, I was struggling with my musical career and could not devote as much time to photography as I would have liked. About eleven years ago, when I was more established and when I moved to California with my wife, Marianne, I started taking photographs in earnest. When we met, Marianne was a fashion model, so it was natural for me to shoot portfolio photographs of her in a small studio in our house, in which I also had darkroom facilities. Before I knew it, the place had turned into one of those quick-print photomats. I would take pictures of Marianne and her model friends; then I'd go off to develop the negatives while they made lunch. Within two or three hours, I would bring back finished prints and get their response. These photo-sessions introduced me to one of photography's greatest rewards: the privilege of seeing and sharing in the pleasure a person derives from looking at a photograph that shows him in his best light.

The ability to capture the essence of a subject, which in a portrait can surface in the subtlety of a smile or the twinkle of an eye, did much to nourish my interest in the art of photography. With time, though, I felt the need to broaden my horizons. Again, Marianne was instrumental. She not only encouraged me to pursue my photography, but helped me chart a whole new direction for what had become an increasingly important part of my life. Around this time, she had learned about John Sexton, a very talented photographer and prominent figure in the Ansel Adams workshops in

Carmel, California. Marianne thought John might be able to offer me something special, so as a Christmas gift, she signed me up for a private two-day workshop in darkroom techniques.

John and I hit it off from the start. I have always been the kind of person who is driven to learn and improve myself, no matter what I do. As I became more involved with photography, I began to have many questions about shooting methods, types of film, and camera formats. I was particularly interested in those technical aspects of developing and printing that would give me more control over the tonal qualities, definition, and mood of the final product — the print. With my curiosity about these fine points of the photographic process, it was natural for me to seek out and learn from an expert like John, who was ideally suited to teach me the things I was interested in knowing.

In retrospect, those early sessions in the darkroom were the beginning of the most intense involvements in the art of photography I've had thus far. But what began as an interest in refining basic printing techniques dovetailed into a whole new appreciation for the zone system, the tonal values of a black-and-white print, as well as for other technical aspects of film processing and printmaking. In the process of teaching me what you can do to a negative *after* you've shot it, John also introduced me to the 4x5 camera, a somewhat cumbersome but very precise apparatus with interchangeable lenses that produces razor-sharp, large-format negatives. "Why don't we go out and shoot some pictures with this thing?" he said to me one day. I must have looked less than enthusiastic because he added, "You know, not everyone is cut out for the 4x5."

At first, I wasn't sure exactly what he meant, but after shooting a few pictures, it was clear. Photographing with this new camera — at least, initially — seemed inconsistent with my life-style, which has always been geared toward finding the fastest, most efficient way of getting something done. It didn't take long for me to figure out that the 4x5 is anything but fast. First, you have to set up a tripod and mount the camera; then

focus and do your tilt adjustments; and then do still more fine-tuning. It's not a snapshot. It's a production — a very slow one at that, and meanwhile, the light keeps changing. Over time, however, I learned these disadvantages of the 4x5 system were far outweighed by the benefits.

After John and I returned from our first day out we went straight into the darkroom and developed the film. At that point, I realized this big negative camera was a far cry from the aim-and-shoot Brownie Hawkeye, the Argus C-3, or any 35mm camera, for that matter. The sharpness and the ability to manipulate perspective and overall quality of individual negatives were unlike anything I had ever seen. Studying them closely, I was amazed at how it was possible to actually see the subtle details and highlights of an entire landscape while the image was still in negative form. And after seeing the prints from that first expedition, I knew that my artistic growth in the field of photography depended on my commitment to this new camera. I've been shooting with it ever since.

Sophisticated and imposing, the 4x5 offered — and demanded — a whole new way of looking at photography. With its swing-and-tilt backs, parallax adjustments, and state-of-the-art optics, this system made available an expanded repertoire of image-making options. A favorite among professionals, the large format gave me a new level of appreciation for composition, balance, and the nuances of light, texture, and shadow. I also discovered that different shooting situations require that I have a wide range of lenses at my disposal. Over time, I have narrowed down my repertoire of lenses to five, from wide-angle to telephoto, and they include a 90mm, 150mm, 210mm, 300mm, and 500mm. I shoot primarily Tri-X film rated at ASA 160 and develop my negatives in HC-110 Kodak Developer.

Henri Cartier-Bresson, the great French photographer of city life, once said the photographer's purpose is "to capture a moment in time." If you delay, even for a second, you can lose that moment. Although Cartier-Bresson was referring primarily to photojournalism, his own area of interest, I think the same applies to photographing the natural landscape. And to me, nothing is more important than drama. Whether I am trying to capture the pulse of light through the arches of a California mission or a majestic sunset off the Point Reyes Peninsula, seizing that moment when light, texture, and shadow come together to make a powerful and cohesive visual statement is the key to the way I approach photography. Time and time again, I have spent hours surveying a scene, especially the movement of light, trying to anticipate when that special moment will come.

I know I have to be ready at that instant when my mind's eye recognizes that the light and shadows are in tune with the elements of the landscape or architectural work I am photographing. In the end, my satisfaction comes, in part, from the realization that I have the technical skills to freeze this singular moment in time on film. But it also derives from knowing that when I stand behind the camera I am there alone, drawing on my most creative resources. Finally, there is the special pleasure that comes from the awareness that, like every photographer, I have a special way of looking at the world; and that my photographs can capture a unique moment — an instant in the life of an alpine meadow, a New England farmhouse, or a snowcapped mountain dotted with pine trees — that will never be seen again or recorded in exactly the same way.

Because I am constantly on the road with my musical career, my shooting schedule is very unpredictable. This has forced me to adopt a different approach than that used by some other photographers. Ansel Adams, whose work I greatly admire, was able to take his mule up into the High Sierra and wait until the light was just right for the shot he wanted, even if it took days. Ansel had the luxury of time. I do not. What I *do* have is the luxury of space — and movement. Rather than waiting for specific lighting conditions, I frequently go out and chase the sun. Once, I shot a picture in California's Yosemite Valley at dawn, packed my gear, boarded a plane, and then shot on the shores of Lake Michigan later that afternoon. On another occasion, when I was filming *Wild Horses,* I flew several hundred miles to photograph the sand dunes of Alamogordo, New Mexico. I arrived just in time. Casting long shadows across the desert's surface, the light was perfect — neither too overcast nor too bright — for highlighting the dramatic contours of windblown sand rippling in gentle swells against the horizon.

One thing I have learned, however, is that planning is often the key to getting good photographs. When we pull into a city, the first thing I do, usually with my assistant, Rob Pincus, is scout out photographic possibilities in surrounding areas. Before we get to our final destination, we do as much research as possible. In this respect, books and guides to the national parks, wilderness areas, and national monuments have been a tremendous asset.

However, many of the finest pictures I have taken are of places I stumbled into literally by accident. Even when I try to do my homework, there are times I come into a city "blind," and have no idea where to begin looking or what there is to see. When performing recently in Akron, Ohio, I asked some of the local people what there was to photograph in the area and was told, ". . . there's really *nothing* to shoot around here."

I found that hard to believe, so we packed the gear and started driving out of town. Just outside the city, we came across a promising stretch of wilderness and decided to explore. It was one of those mornings; the air was cold and the ground was still spongy from last night's rain. We set out at random and, before long, we found some great photographic opportunities. At Blue Hen Falls I was struck by the simple sheet of water seemingly frozen over an outcropping of rock. We walked down the path a way, and as I pushed through the underbrush I saw Brandywine Falls. I was amazed at what some people call *nothing* . . . it was beautiful. Here was an entire universe of virginal beauty that through my photographs I would be able to share with others. It never ceases to amaze me how much there is to see, if you just take the time to look.

That experience also taught me how little some people know about their own areas. Everyone can tell you about the spectacular sights in Death Valley or the Grand Canyon, but too few people ever take the trouble to search out the beauty in their own backyards. Photography trains the eye to see in a completely new way; it can reveal an entirely new world of mystery and fascination in what we assumed was ordinary, familiar, and uninteresting. For the most part, I set out to photograph landscapes in our great national parks, only to discover that some of the most inspiring sites were in little-known places outside such cities as Akron, Ohio, and Duluth, Minnesota, and Albuquerque, New Mexico.

The extraordinary diversity of America's natural landscape has kept my vision fresh and helped me maintain my enthusiasm for making photographs. The road, of course, is a never-ending source of photographic stimulation. In fact, there is nothing like traveling on America's highways to help a person steer clear of photographic ruts. No matter where I am, I seem to always find some aspect of the landscape that is worthy of a permanent place on film. I can remember the excitement of shooting giant tufts of clouds in the Southern California sky. And the time I photographed a cemetery; I was touched, I guess, and a little saddened by this graveyard, which represented the lives of so many people, now totally unattended and overgrown.

Despite the temptation to stop and record every compelling sight, I have had a tendency to focus on certain themes for limited stretches of time. Depending on the part of the country through which I am touring, I will explore a particular subject — geological formations, farm scenes, or moving water — until I can shoot it to my satisfaction. These intense periods of concentration have produced some of what I think is my best work and led to some of the most rewarding experiences I've had with my camera.

When I am ready to begin shooting in an area, the first thing I do is go out and just start looking. I look at form, design, texture, and organization. In a city, I may notice the way stepped-back skyscrapers stack up against the sky or the abstract patterns formed on the walls of old buildings by brick, crumbling mortar, and peeling paint. But photographing people is an entirely different matter. I tend to look for people who have strong faces. I have always believed the eyes are the key to photographing people — that's where the drama shows. Although composition, balance, and tonal values are still essential ingredients to the final image, I have found that other, more personal values, many of which also come out in my music, take precedence. I once met a man who told me the way to understand other people in your life is to accept the fact that when there is no drama, man will create it because he needs this excitement. Some individuals create negative drama, while others create positive drama. It is a question of which way they want their lives to go.

I feel these elements of drama exist in my photograph of people like Bob and Harry, two residents of New York City's Bowery. I remember, at first glance, their situation was anything but positive. They were down and out in the Bowery. But when I told Harry we would like to take his picture, he was so genuinely excited that he pushed back his hair, buttoned up his shirt, pulled up his socks, and proudly squared his shoulders to face the camera. The same was true with the man we affectionately came to call "Mike in the Box." He wanted his picture made, but only after he could establish the few ingredients that constituted dignity to *him*.

The excitement of shooting film in the field is only half the story. Photography involves two stages: first, recording the instant when your eye sees the dramatic potential of the picture, and second, transforming that vision into a final image. For me, the real fulfillment comes in the darkroom. In this respect, I see printing as the last and best act in this overall process. To print a photograph, study it, and then realize, "This is exactly what I thought it was going to be," is very rewarding. Rarely does life give you the opportunity to have that kind of control over the outcome of your work.

Like any creative project in which I have become deeply involved, photographing America has brought me face to face with a whole new set of challenges. At times, I felt I had lost my "creative eye" and there was nothing to shoot. Then John Sexton gave me a very valuable piece of advice. He sent me a telegram saying, "Shoot what you like and you will like what you shoot." I have found that to be true.

I became aware that what excited me most about photography was being able to capture organization according to my own vision. Design represents organization. Organization represents lack of chaos. And, more important, it is a way of unifying and bringing into balance a set of seemingly disconnected elements. This principle has always had great importance in my life and, more recently, has become central to the way I approach everything.

Being aware of the organizational elements in an untouched landscape has become more of a reflex lately — a sort of photographic "software" that is now a part of my mind's eye. For example, if I am driving through Oregon's Columbia River gorge and see a line of Douglas fir trees rimming the canyon wall, I will stack these elements in my eye, make note of critical highlights and shadows, and try to compose these into a format consistent with the dimensions of whatever camera I'm using. I will also look for a "visual hook" that will center the photograph and locate the viewer in the image. If the trees, canyon walls, and other elements in the scene create a dramatic image, I will stop. If not, I just keep moving.

The collection of photographs in this book represents the governing principles of design and organization as I feel them. I have found these qualities consistently throughout the American landscape. Like Ansel Adams, I have tried to photograph nature, when possible, the way it *could* have been, before the telephone wires, roads, steel cables, and, most damaging of all, people who don't care, appeared. Photographing the American wilderness from this perspective has brought me in touch with the timeless quality of nature and with the reali-zation that we are all just temporary visitors on this planet. I particularly felt this in the gnarled and twisted roots of a Florida cypress tree, in the staircase of water falling over rocks in Georgia's untouched DeSoto Falls, and in nature's delicate arrangement of water lilies in the Okefenokee Swamp.

American cities, with their busy streets, soaring towers, and other individual testimonials to technological wizardry, pay their own special tributes to design and organization. Since it is light that gives architectural spaces their full value, the camera is ideally suited to document these elements. I have seen this at work in the steel cables spanning suspension bridges in Manhattan and San Francisco, in the powerful geometries of crisscrossing superhighways, and in the play of light and shadow against terra-cotta columns or the arches of the San Miguel Mission. And last but not least, there are trainyards. Maybe it's because I've heard so many Johnny Cash songs, but I have always been attracted to trainyards.

One of the greatest pleasures I have had doing this project has been learning more about light — its moods, its power, and its capacity for changing, sometimes in a matter of seconds, the entire face of a natural landscape. In fact, nothing has helped me more than photography to appreciate the way in which light can help us read the mysterious face of nature. By the light of the setting sun, the striations of a canyon wall reveal crisp traces of thousands of years of wear and tear and natural evolution. And I remember the sand dunes outside Beatty, Nevada, when a ray of light cutting through the overcast sky brought out tracks of a small beetle, changing the mood from one of desolation to life and vitality.

Like any photographer, I am partial to some lighting conditions over others. Although early morning light starts out good, as the day progresses, it gradually deteriorates. When shooting in the morning, I usually find that by the time I have set up my equipment, the shadows have become harder, the light has intensified, and the subtleties have begun to fade. This doesn't happen in late afternoon. When you see something you like in the evening light, you can count on it to get better with time. The shadows get longer and the light gets softer.

Traveling on the road for the past year has given me a whole new perspective on this country. There are features in the urban and rural landscape that I would never have seen had I not intentionally gone out looking for photographs, and just having the camera at my side has made life more exciting. For years, I shot almost exclusively indoors, in the studio, doing fashion photography and portraits. I had complete control of the lighting conditions, models, and other technical aspects of the photographic shoot. In general, though, I found myself snapping a lot of pictures and feeling that in the end I would come up with something good. Of course, shooting landscapes has changed much of that. I have had to adjust to working with what is given, to take my cue from the specific conditions of a setting. I was truly out of control of the elements I had always counted on. Whereas before I would try to inject life into an artificial composition, now I had to learn to photograph the world as I found it.

This reorientation has opened up a whole new level of visual perception. No matter where or how I am traveling, I am always visually scouring the landscape for photographic possibilities. I have found myself mentally composing pictures under the most extreme and bizarre conditions — in a helicopter hovering at eight thousand feet above the lunar landscape of Mono Lake or cruising on an interstate at eighty miles an hour past a sheep ranch outside Traverse City, Michigan. I have discovered that long before I even take the picture, I am already beginning to imagine the problems I am likely to encounter in shooting and printing it.

Photography is unique in my life because it is the only thing that brings me in contact with the past and that links me to the continuum of history. I have always tended to be so future-oriented that I never really concerned myself with what had happened in the past. It seemed that the past was something I could not change,

but the future could always be altered if I really applied myself to the task.

To stand behind my camera in Yosemite Valley and see one of America's most awesome landscapes come into focus on the ground glass fills me with a newfound respect for time. To have heard about it is one thing. But you cannot disregard it once you have seen a sunset edge the ancient canyon rims of Yosemite Valley with a golden glow. These geological landmarks have been in the process of formation for hundreds of thousands of years, long enough to make you realize how unimportant we all are in the grand scheme of things — and how timeless and enduring the monuments of our natural landscape are.

A photographer once said that the difference between a photograph and a snapshot is the perspective from which you take it. The importance of this comment did not register when I first read it, but after a year of shooting America I have come to see how profound this observation is. I had the opportunity to photograph Niagara Falls from a spot where I'm sure no mortal man has been before. As I was walking around the top of the falls looking for a novel vantage point, a busload of tourists spotted me and started to head my way. If I had hoped for a quiet moment in which to compose my shot, this was not going to be it. I was going to have to find a less crowded spot. At that point, a security guard came up to me and I asked, "Are there any places to shoot the falls without all the people and wires crossing into the frame?" Pointing to a spot deep below the falls, he said, "Follow me," and we traipsed down into the canyon. Looking at and listening to the thunderous waters from below rather than from above cast the familiar sight of Niagara Falls into an entirely different light.

Of course, it is not always possible to photograph from unusual vantage points. In a place like Yosemite Valley it may not even be necessary to go off the beaten track. Yosemite is in my mind filled with the "greatest hits of photography." In short, it is awesome, a word I seldom use. Most of the shots I took there are from designated photographic points. Half Dome, Bridalveil Falls, and El Capitan have probably been photographed thousands of times, but the great thing is that each shot is different. Because each visual moment — and the person viewing it from behind his camera — is different.

There is no question that photography has been an extension of my creative self, but it has also offered me an escape — a refuge of sorts — from the intense scrutiny of the public eye and the pandemonium of a packed concert hall. There is something very special about being alone and composing a picture in one of America's vast — and vacant — natural amphitheaters. For a change, I am looking out but no one is looking in, and I am in control of the only picture-making machine within miles. When I am finally away from the glitter and the lights, there is a rare moment of privacy when I can relax and not worry about how I'm dressed, or how my hair looks, or the way my voice sounds.

Photographing in the wilderness has also given me a chance to see things which, because of the pace and pressure of live performances, I may not have seen. Once when I was driving along a riverbank near Sheridan, Wyoming, I saw a beautifully backlit tree. I pointed it out to Rob and said, "Look at the way the light outlines those branches. You know, before I started photography, I could have passed this tree a thousand times and never seen it." Photography opens up new vistas and feelings that you would otherwise miss altogether.

In the photographic chronicle that follows, I have tried to capture the rich and complex character of America's most photographable assets. As a result, an unusual juxtaposition sometimes occurs between single photographs or groupings of images. For example, you may find a Japanese rock garden on one page, a prisoner from Lexington, Georgia, on the next, and a bristling city skyline on yet another page. I think this is good. Over time, I have become aware that these alternating points of view reflect my own shooting style, which is one that emphasizes discovery, exploration, and a need

to chronicle many different facets of American life.

As I think about how photography has influenced me over the past several years, I am reminded of a story about Ansel Adams. When, as a young boy, he gave up a budding career as a performing pianist and bought himself his first camera, his mother warned, "Ansel, don't you know that the camera can't express the soul?" To which the young Ansel responded, "Yes, but the photographer can." I could not agree more. To those of you, then, who do not yet have a camera, my advice is go out and buy one — any camera — and start to see the country. You won't really begin to see America until you start photographing it.

We were outside Tacoma, Washington, in a helicopter when I saw this bed of big rocks. I asked the pilot to drop down so I could shoot this scene. I loved the way the rocks in the foreground led directly back up the mountain, as if they had rolled off the peak. The eddies of water swirling around the central boulder gave this landscape a point of intense activity that keeps the image from being too static.

When John Sexton saw this photograph, the first thing he noticed was the edge of the asphalt road in the foreground. He was sure I had accidentally jarred the tripod, tilting the camera out of position. I had a hard time convincing him that I had intentionally included this element in the frame. The best photographs I have ever seen are those in which the viewer is allowed a personal reference point that indicates where in the scene the photograph is being taken as well as what lies beyond that frame of reference. In this, the texture of the asphalt road and the spiky grasses at the rim of the canyon provide what I call "additional information" that helps tell the total story of this landscape. John thought this over for a while and, eventually, decided that maybe I knew what I was doing after all.

SAND DUNE, WHITE SANDS NATIONAL MONUMENT, NEW MEXICO

I have always been drawn to the serenity and remoteness of desert landscapes. White Sands National Monument offers some of the most dramatic juxtapositions of sand, shadow, and sky in the country. In this photograph, I was interested in capturing the flowing contours of stark desert shadows sandwiched between a thick, fleecy sky and rippling dunes. Unfortunately the sunlight doesn't always cooperate, and it took several visits to this site to produce an image that pleased me.

VENTURA FARMS, HIDDEN VALLEY, CALIFORNIA

In this small valley in Southern California, there are thousands of great oak trees. The sense of the mountain in the back is very important to the depth in this photograph.

When I am at my farm near Athens, Georgia, I can spend hours watching the clouds. I have always liked the end of the day when, as the sun descends, the clouds change from a fiery red-orange to soft shades of cool magenta. Here the natural elements seem to be tailor-made for each other. The clouds, treetops, and gently sloping meadow are layered into an arrangement of complementary domes.

OLD CATTLE PENS, CLAYTON, GEORGIA

I pass this scene near my farm many times. It is always peaceful.

The sheriff in Lexington, Georgia, is a friend of mine. I told him I was looking for people with great faces and hands to photograph. So he took me to see Musrite, who turned out to be a classic character. Musrite was an old bluesman from Georgia who played songs by Muddy Waters and Gatemouth Brown. Sitting on the sofa in front of his house, he strummed his guitar and sang for me.

I'm ashamed to say I used to spend countless Sundays sitting in this church, thinking how much I would like to photograph its architecture. But when I came here alone, without any other members of the congregation present, I noticed it had a totally different feel. Under these conditions, the quiet, simple space took on a new sanctity. The janitor who was tidying up was an important part of that experience.

On the way from the Duluth airport to my hotel, I saw the converging lines of this superhighway. So I got up at six o'clock the next morning, loaded film, and prepared my camera gear. Because of the crowds and traffic snarls I anticipated, I asked Rob Pincus, my assistant, to see if we could get a police escort for the shoot. The local authorities were more than happy to help. They explained, however, that the bridge had just opened the day before and that I shouldn't count on getting any photographs of it without automobiles streaming across. My impression was that they were expecting a major traffic jam. I decided to take my chances. I was on the bridge shooting for forty-five minutes. There were several policemen on hand to make sure everything went smoothly. And it did. Only two cars drove across the bridge the entire time. I'm not sure they needed this bridge as much as they thought.

With its long, stark shadows and wrinkled dunes dotted with sagebrush, the Nevada desert is a beautiful sight. This is especially true in the early evening, when the red-tinged rays just before sunset create dramatic effects with the cloud-mottled skies and swells of hourglass-fine sand. When I encounter an environment as extreme and vast as the desert, I think of great American pioneers and how driven they must have been to cross terrain such as this without having any idea of what was on the other side or, for that matter, how long the desert stretched. These American explorers were driven by progress and hope for a better future. And for their courage, I admire them.

It was a rainy day on Mono Lake. I was shooting in the middle of bizarre crystalline formations called tufa, which, I was told, millions of years ago had been submerged beneath the lake's surface. From the outset, it was clear why, over the years, Hollywood movie studios had filmed scenes for science fiction movies at this location. After aeons of geological wear and tear, the receding waters had etched intricate patterns into the rock faces. There was something about this eerie setting that suggested the lost city of a fabulous kingdom.

CRYSTALLINE FORMATION, MONO LAKE, CALIFORNIA

We landed the helicopter at an out-of-the-way sheep ranch. I asked the shepherd, an old Basque, if I could take a picture of him with his flock of two thousand sheep. He was happy to oblige, or so I thought. I explained that I wanted him to stand squarely in the middle of his flock, but he misunderstood and walked all the way around the field until he was completely out of the frame. In the process of circling his flock, he inadvertently herded all the animals into a tightly packed cluster of wall-to-wall sheep. I took the photograph anyway. I'm glad I did, since from the look of at least one of the sheep, someone seemed to know what I was after.

ALPINE VEGETATION, SIERRA NEVADA, CALIFORNIA

I was up in the mountains chasing after clouds when
I came across a dense bed of alpine growth. The leaves
were so thick and rubbery they made me think of those
loud plastic flowers you can buy by the cartload at any
five-and-dime.

It was one of those gloomy days. We were in a helicopter circling high above the Sierra. I saw a massive ridge of granite that I wanted to photograph and asked the pilot to bring us down within good shooting range. So he landed on a "saddleback," a flat, narrow perch of rock no more than fifteen feet long in any one direction. I stepped onto the ridge and set up my equipment in the gusting wind. If I thought I would feel secure with fifteen feet of solid ground beneath my feet, I was dead wrong. Looking down at an eight-thousand-foot drop on all sides made me as scared as I've ever been in my life. My knees started to shake, but I managed to take my photograph and run. Back to the helicopter, that is. Once inside, I felt much more secure until the pilot told me that the reason he had parked the chopper on the saddleback was so that if he lost power on takeoff, he could regain it by letting the updraft coming up the slope start the blades spinning. As we lifted off, I thought of Ansel Adams, who would have taken days to climb to these remote places for that one unique photograph. And I had just dropped in from a helicopter. I thought to myself, "Nothing is sacred anymore."

When you are filming a movie, there is a lot of downtime to fill. They told me I had a couple of hours to kill one day during *Wild Horses,* so I rounded up some real cowboys — not the Hollywood kind — for a group portrait. The guys really ended up liking this shot. As for the dog, he was the perfect model. The next day, these cowhands were rounding up horses. I liked the pattern of the light and dark animals as they were milling around the corral. I climbed up on top of the barn and took a quick shot. I was glad I worked fast, because by the time I loaded another film holder into the camera someone had spooked the horses and they had all taken off.

HORSE ROUNDUP, SHERIDAN, WYOMING

As unsavory as this bunch looks, these guys are actually some of the finest people I know. The man on the far left standing in the doorway is Bill Richards, one of my airplane pilots. The patriarch sitting in the chair with the cane is my older brother, Leland. The guy with the black hat in the window is another pilot, Bill Matto. The bank robber with the white mustache is Allan Hill, my mother's bus driver (I bought my mother a bus because she likes to go on tour with us). And the guy sitting on the porch with the knife in his hand is my younger brother, Roy. So never believe that what you see is what you get.

ALPINE LAKE, SHERIDAN, WYOMING

After a morning on the set of *Wild Horses,* I drove into the mountains to photograph this alpine lake. It stopped snowing about an hour before I set up my camera. The sky had already cleared and the flurry had crowned the virgin pines with a layer of powder, giving this forest the look of a thousand Christmas trees. As it turned out, my timing could not have been better. I managed to catch the last rays of the sun as they grazed the tips of the pines. The combination of sunshine, the glassy stillness of the lake, and the crystalline snow made for a very special moment.

One afternoon, high in the mountains outside Sheridan, Wyoming, a light snow had just fallen and fresh clouds were already beginning to gather in the sky. It looked like a storm was coming, but I decided to go out shooting anyway. Prowling along the riverbank, I came across this luminous white bridge. In the distance, a solitary peacock opened and closed its magnificent tail plumage.

I have passed this house a thousand times and every time I see it, I am amazed at how different it looks. It seems to change entirely, depending on the time of year. The moss on which it sits is actually a plant called the kudzu vine. It was brought from China to stop erosion — which it did. In fact, it took so well to the Georgia soil that it has slowly taken over the state. You just can't kill the stuff. You can't burn it, you can't poison it. In the summer, this ramshackle house is so overgrown with kudzu that you can only see its roof.

KUDZU VINE, SPRING, ATHENS, GEORGIA

FATHER AND SON, MADISON, GEORGIA

TEXTURED WOOD, OLD HOUSE, BLAIRSVILLE, GEORGIA

It was eleven o'clock Sunday morning on the south side of Chicago. All the churches were full, and the streets were empty. We were cruising in a limo, looking for something to shoot. We were completely lost and had no idea where we were going. These hubcaps on a chain-link fence caught my eye. Rob and I set up the camera on the sidewalk and started shooting. Two guys who worked in this junkyard said, "Hey, put me in the movies, Jack." I don't think we would have gotten out of this neighborhood with our camera if it wasn't for a policeman driving by who recognized me. He said, "With that kind of camera equipment around here, you need a police escort." It turned out he was a real photography buff, so we talked shop.

From the way these tombstones were arranged, I was sure that this cemetery was originally intended as a war memorial. And, in fact, it may very well have been. But I noticed that all the headstones with women's names were turned backward. Perhaps these were family plots. I was particularly struck by the black wreath on one tombstone. It seemed so final.

When I think of the Great Plains, I think of dazzling sunsets. I think of grain elevators and railroad tracks. Train tracks are the last fixtures of what Thomas Wolfe called "the place of huge stillness . . . where young men are drunk with the bite and sparkle of air and mad with solar energy." I think this reminded me of Crock-ett, Texas, a sparsely populated rural outpost where I used to spend summers as a young boy. I love the stillness in such out-of-the-way places, a quietude that is unique to people who are simple, honest, and go on about their own business.

I was pushing my luck to get this shot. The sun was sinking fast. Within seconds, it seemed, light was suddenly in scarce supply. But this was the least of my problems. It was nine o'clock in the evening and the show where I was to perform had already started. By the time I was ready to shoot, the second act was performing, which meant I had to be on stage in less than an hour! I was also very concerned that I had not even been to the concert hall, so I had no idea how far I had to drive to get there. But I was determined to shoot this photograph. And shoot it right. Although this cascade is just a small part of Sioux Falls, I liked the look of the rushing current and the way this staircase of water, over time, had gouged a deep path for itself through the rocks. Fortunately, I managed to take this picture and make it on stage in time for my opening number.

As close as I live to the ocean in Los Angeles, over the years I have spent surprisingly little time on the beach. Recently, however, I have found myself increasingly drawn to the coastline, trying to better understand its attraction. Of all the coastal landscapes I have seen, Half Moon Bay is one of my favorites. Studying the rocks near the shoreline, I couldn't help but be intrigued by the face-off between land and water, where two titanic forces — one stationary and one in motion — are engaged in eternal dispute. In these photographs, the power of these forces is suggested by the turbulence of the ocean and, opposing it, the formidable natural seawall that protects the land from constant erosion. I have always wanted to photograph "The Thumb," a giant rock bursting out of the water near Half Moon Bay. One day I left San Francisco at 4:30 in the morning, so I would be there in time for the proper light. When I arrived, the moon was setting. As I was getting my camera ready, the rocks were still shrouded in shadows. Then, the sun sneaked over the foothills of the coastal range. The sun's glow kindled the start of another day, revealing seagulls nesting on rocks in the distance and the angry surf washing against this luminous rock.

The lush green ferns and backlit leaves, which look like they have a thin coating of snowflakes, pay tribute to many different layers of the forest environment. This image represents a big step forward for me photographically, since it was while shooting this scene that I first applied what John Sexton had taught me about expansion and contraction of black-and-white negatives. Put simply, this is a technique that permits a photographer to amplify or subdue details in a landscape that is shot under extreme lighting conditions. In this case, the harsh light of high noon created an extraordinary range of tonal values. Without contracting the tones of this forest scene — which is accomplished by overexposing and then underdeveloping the negative — it would have been impossible to capture the highlights in the stark white zones of the reflective vegetation and the subtle textures buried within ground shadow. I particularly like the dirt road that appears to stop at the top of the hill and gives little hint of what lies beyond.

THE GOLDEN GATE BRIDGE, SAN FRANCISCO, CALIFORNIA

This well-known monument is easily recognized by the long span of its steel cables. This photograph was shot from the Sausalito side of the Golden Gate Bridge and the early morning fog is just dense enough to conceal all traces of San Francisco's bustling urban civilization. The rock in the foreground combined with the weather conditions gives the Golden Gate the appearance of being a bridge to nowhere.

Cactuses, cottonwoods, and canyon walls made of sandstone created a picturebook setting for this remote California mission. In the blazing afternoon light, the chalky plaster walls of this old well shone white as a rattlesnake skeleton bleached by the hot sun. When I took this photograph, I felt like I was going back in time more than a hundred years. I imagined cowboys riding up to the front of the mission and leading their horses to the well for a drink, and padres inviting them into the cool inner sanctum of their desert retreat.

A large bell serves as the focal point for the San Miguel Mission. With its alternating zones of shadow and light, the descending row of arches creates an abstract — and very graphic — pattern of scalloping. These architectual forces are further strengthened by curved benches. The sharply raked light of midday accents the strong grid pattern of the tilework and the layer of brick that has been exposed beneath the crumbling stucco exterior. As striking as these architectural lines are, I have often wished I had taken this photograph with a monk sitting on one of the shaded benches.

As I was driving back from the San Miguel Mission, I was drawn to the long branches of several oak trees reaching out and almost touching the feathery tips of a grassy meadow. As it passed over the grass, the sun gave it such a luminous texture that I almost seemed to be looking through a tunnel of light. Against this radiance, shimmering halolike on the field, a delicate network of branches floated across the sky like a piece of black lace.

BRANDYWINE FALLS, AKRON, OHIO

Going on a photography expedition is a little like going on a hunt. And taking risks is a big part of the fun. Of course, things don't always go smoothly, as was the case for this photograph of Brandywine Falls. Rob and I were hiking in a magnificent forest outside Akron, Ohio. At one point, we had to climb down a steep rock and descend into the falls. I had the tripod and Rob was carrying a huge bag with the 4x5 camera and film packs. I went over first and started down a narrow trail that led toward the falls. Then something strange happened. I knew I had seen Rob come over the rock, but when I looked around, I couldn't find him. I thought he might have gone back to the car to get something. I started to scream, "Rob!" at the top of my voice. There was no answer. The waterfall was deafening. Then I turned around, looked down, and saw Rob lying a hundred and fifty feet below me at the bottom of Brandywine Falls. Actually, all I could see was this little red shirt in a tangle of shrubs. I started laughing so hard because I knew from his waving that everything was all right. It took us thirty minutes to get hooked up again. Fortunately, there was a shelf just beyond the rock that kept my camera bag from going over.

As we were driving around Akron, Ohio, we kept stopping and asking people if there was anything interesting to photograph in the area. We kept getting the same answer: "There is nothing to shoot here." Finally, we saw a sign that said Virginia Kendall Park and decided to make our way there. It was almost night when we stumbled into the side of this hill. This photograph happens to be a two-minute exposure. Most of all, I was drawn to the network of roots that reached, like grasping fingers, into the sloping earth. We had to do a little gardening before we could photograph the next shot at Blue Hen Falls. The place was littered with beer cans and candy wrappers, which we removed to restore the spot to its pristine beauty. It angered me that people would leave rubbish in a place as special as this.

BLUE HEN FALLS, AKRON, OHIO

Pemaquid Point, near the end of the Bristol peninsula, is one of the most photographed spots on the Maine coast. A heavy surf breaks almost constantly against the ledges here and the firs and spruces grow to the high-tide line.

I went to shoot Niagara Falls on my birthday. And I wanted a really special shot. I met a guard at the top of the falls who offered to show me some good vantage points. I said, "Please don't give me the routine shots. Let's go somewhere where I can shoot the falls so it will be obvious that this is one of the Seven Wonders of the World." Without a moment's hesitation, the guard pointed straight down at the base of the falls and said, "Follow me." So we climbed down two hundred feet through the swirling mist and spray, watching our feet every step of the way until we got to the bottom. As the next photograph shows, the first thing I saw when I looked up were two pieces of wood that had fallen into the shape of a cross. It really stunned me.

TRAIN TRACKS, ATHENS, GEORGIA

I love the geometry of train tracks. I like the parallel lines of steel rails, embedded in gravel, trailing off into infinity. They make me think of America on the road. Rails. They make me think of trainyards. Maybe I have heard too many Johnny Cash songs, but I still love trainyards.

As I was driving on my farm, I came across these backlit trees against a beautiful wooden fence. I wanted to capture the full impact of the lacy branches and the running fence.

This is Georgia's answer to Mount Rushmore. The granite face on which Generals Lee, Grant, and Jackson are carved is more than a thousand feet high. You get some idea of the scale of this gigantic bas-relief from the tall pines growing along its face. A six-foot man can stand up straight inside the horse's mouth. When this memorial was finished, four of the men who had worked on it hauled a picnic table onto General Grant's shoulder, sat down, and ate lunch.

There is nothing like a gravestone, a few strands of fog, and a full moon to create a scene that looks like something out of a werewolf movie.

For many people who spend long stretches of time in jail, the cell becomes their home. I saw this pair of hands coming through the bars of a jail cell. There was something almost comfortable about the way this man had placed the cigarettes and lighter on the crossbar of the cell. These pieces of personal property told a story. They seemed to say: "This is where I am. This is my home, at least for now."

The workmen were scraping layers of paint from these columns. They said, "Even General Sherman couldn't have burned down this house if he'd tried."

I like the abstract patterns an ordinary material like gravel forms.

OKEFENOKEE SWAMP, GEORGIA

I flew by helicopter to a remote section of the Okefenokee Swamp. On the basis of movies I had seen of the Florida Everglades, I had painted a very vivid image in my mind of what I might encounter in the vast swamplands of southern Georgia. I imagined a gothic rainforest teeming with mangroves, arching branches, and other lush floral trimmings. What I actually found was something less hospitable, but every bit as magical. I had brought my 4x5 camera, but it was impossible to set up a tripod in the boggy terrain. As a result, I had to use a 35mm camera for the entire expedition. The swamp water was black as crude oil and a wall of densely packed trees formed the perimeter of what appeared to be an impenetrable forest. I was particularly drawn to the lanky tubular roots of the trees, the clumps of floating lilies, and the water reeds, all of which stood out against the dark stagnant water. As I made my way by boat, I noticed rows of soggy wooden stumps poking through the water's surface. They were the skeletal remains of an old railroad. Years ago, an ambitious lumber magnate had built an elaborate system of elevated tracks and trestles that wound deep into the heart of these hostile swamplands. It was hard to believe that trains had actually slinked along these rails carrying Okefenokee's rich harvest of lumber.

When I saw this farmhouse, I pulled over and stopped. From a distance I had been drawn to the unusual shapes and stacking arrangement of the domed silos and tri-angular rooftops. But close up, I was just as fascinated by the weathered advertisement for WKTY radio. With its bold comic-book character and sun-bleached paint curling off the shed's siding, this sign was a classic example of rural Americana. The fractured quality of these flakes reminded me of early photographs by Aaron Siskind.

I pulled my car into the driveway and set up the camera. While I was making my final adjustments, the owner stormed out the front door in a rage, demanding to know what I was doing. As the man got closer, he recognized me and turned white as a sheet. I think he was embarrassed about some of the things he had shouted at me on his way out. After we started talking, though, he happily consented to letting me photograph the barn, but only if I agreed to come inside and meet his wife. Once inside, I discovered that she had just given birth to a baby boy the day before. They took pictures of me holding the baby and everyone had a great time. I was especially pleased that this situation, which began on shaky ground, ended up being a very positive experience for all of us.

Lake Michigan's deep blue color and turbulence confirmed something I had always suspected — that these
large inland bodies of water are potentially every bit as
powerful and dangerous as the ocean itself. I took one-
second exposures to capture the movement of the water
undercutting the shoreline in these two pictures. Exposed tree roots, snaking over rocks and porous soil,
reminded me of motifs in Oriental paintings. As for the
layered slate cliffs, they looked almost man-made and
recalled the carefully laid stone walls of an ancient city.

I had just found out that the band had been invited to tour Japan. In preparation for this trip, I wanted to learn more about the Japanese, especially their unique sense of space, light, and texture. So I visited the Japanese Gardens at UCLA, which has some beautiful examples of miniaturized landscapes and rock gardens, as these photographs show. The Japanese have a special talent for creating serene retreats. I remember distinctly that there was a gentleness everywhere in this man-made landscape. I could see it in the water that trickled into a pool and in the arrangement of water lilies. Even carp swimming beneath the surface were important elements of the pervasive tranquility. Stopping at a small grotto, I was intrigued by the rock paving, and by the interplay of light and dark boulders with bamboo leaves and bonsai trees.

I took this photograph of a Japanese cemetery shortly after being on tour in Japan. During my stay there, I was especially impressed with the ability of the Japanese to take a small space and get so much into it. Although the burial plots are crammed together, the families have spared no expense in commemorating their loved ones. They have given this cemetery a sense of organization and dignity. Watching over the proceedings, a large branching tree, reminiscent of arboreal motifs used in Japanese screens, adds a calligraphic character to the entire landscape.

STRIATED ROCK, OAHU, HAWAII

I was standing on a road that goes nowhere and stops in midair over the central lanes of Manhattan Bridge. From here, I had an unusual vantage point from which to shoot the urban landscape that, at first glance, looks like it came straight out of Paris. Of course, the billboard that reads "Winston. America's Best" gives it away. Nevertheless, there is still something about the architecture, which is out of another era, and the aging trucks that creates the impression that this scene was photographed decades ago. I considered airbrushing the trash out of the side of the road, but decided it should stay. After all, messy vitality is what this whole area is about.

Buildings and bridges are the structural signposts with which a great city claims its place in the popular imagination. While everyone is free to shut off the television set or walk out of a concert, no one can close his eyes to the works of architecture that define the stage of urban life. In the case of Manhattan, that stage is an eye-popping collage of slick, gleaming skyscrapers, gothic towers, and spidery steel cables that hold up the Brook-lyn Bridge. Here the Brooklyn Bridge is more than a link between two boroughs; it is a dividing line that separates the old from the new. The colony of soggy pilings in the foreground looks like the remains of another, much more primitive, city that made way for those future-oriented behemoths on the far side of the bridge.

Mike is his name — he sleeps in a box. He is also a classic slice of New York.

Harry and Bob were down and out on the Bowery. But when I told them I would like to take their photograph, Harry pushed back his hair, buttoned his shirt, pulled up his socks, and proudly squared his shoulders. I believe all men have an innate dignity.

They must have been in a really big hurry to get this bridge fixed, because it was two o'clock in the morning when I passed this work brigade. By the time I decided I wanted to photograph this scene, it was too late. I had already crossed the bridge and had to turn around. But the traffic was so backed up it took me almost half an hour to circle back. I used a relatively long lens because I didn't want the men to see me photographing them. I wanted to catch them going about their work without posing. Silhouetted against the eerie spotlights and steamy vapor, they looked like something out of *2001*. Once I finished the shot, word got out that I was there and most of the guys stopped what they were doing and came over. I ended up paying for this photograph in autographs.

I set up this composition of fencing materials as a study in light and texture. I used Techpan film to accentuate the contrast between the corrugated sheet metal and the roll of chicken wire.

I especially enjoy shooting photographs when I'm with Marianne and my son Christopher. For one thing, it takes some pressure off me, because I don't feel like I'm depriving them of family time. Besides, a photographic expedition is something we can usually all enjoy together. Unlike many entertainers, I try not to stay on the road for extended periods of time. When I am performing in cities near my farm in Athens, Georgia, I will fly home each night so I can spend time with my family. This gives me an opportunity to look at an environment, such as this lake on our farm, that I will have a chance to shoot on more than one occasion.

ABSTRACT WATER, WATSON MILL BRIDGE, GEORGIA

With its bizarre sandstone formations and huge rocks jutting out of nowhere, Zion National Park is filled with some of America's eeriest and most spectacular landscapes. Among the park's geological treasures is the Great White Throne, a monolithic formation that has been the subject for some of the world's greatest photographers. Oddly enough, I took this picture from a designated photographic viewpoint. There, a plaque instructs the traveler that the Great White Throne is one of the most photographed rocks in the United States, and that it represents a special challenge for those who wish to shoot it properly. The weather, which can change without notice, is just one of many problems the photographer is likely to encounter. Among others, disruptive shadows cast by adjacent rocks early in the day tend to obscure subtle features of the lower elevations. In short, photographing this natural wonder can be a nightmare. But when I was there I felt very fortunate because the sky was spotless, the alpine forests of the valley were well illuminated, and a fresh layer of snow had just coated the higher elevations of the Throne, giving it an iceberg sheen.

This scene set up a powerful contrast between a living tree and a mass of inert rock. I liked the way that all the stress marks in the rocks give the appearance of leading to that solitary tree crowning the ridge.

It was snowing. I was driving through the canyons of Zion National Park with Marianne and Christopher at my side. The sun was making its final descent behind one of the park's magnificent sandstone ridges. There were long crisp shadows everywhere and the deep orange spires cut a dramatic spine between the white snow and the electric blue backdrop of sunset. Struck by the beautiful shades of orange and unusual outcroppings of rock, Marianne turned to me and said, "Why don't we stop so you can take some pictures?" So we pulled over to the side of the road. Dumping me like a hot potato, Christopher bolted out of the van and made a beeline for a snowbank, with Marianne following. Meanwhile, Rob and I unloaded the camera and started photographing just in time to catch the moon rising over the horizon. Suddenly, the entire landscape was set aglow by the last rays of the setting sun. And while I brought the moon into focus on the ground glass for this picture, I remember thinking: "This landscape looks like the lunar surface. For all I know, I could be standing on the moon looking back at the earth."

I have a housekeeper in Athens, Georgia, who has lived in this area all her life. Whenever I am after something unique, she's the first I ask for advice. She told me about Lewis Russell, a gamecock breeder in Comer, Georgia. It is illegal to fight gamecocks in the United States, but not to breed them for export. Lewis raises and trains about forty of these birds at a time and then sells them to be taken across the border to Mexico. The moment I set eyes on Lewis, who had been born and raised on this piece of property, I wanted to shoot him in his natural environment, against the haylofts and old plows. But I never got that far. As we stood around chatting, he said: "You know what you ought to do? You ought to get my wife out here and watch her churn butter." She came out of the house and her hair was in rollers. "Oh, dear," she said. "Should I take these rollers out of my hair?" I said, "It's up to you, but as far as I'm concerned I'd rather you keep them." So she did. It's funny how, for me, those rollers stood for a whole way of life that is just about gone. I remember the last time I saw my grandmother, which was twenty-five years ago. She had rollers in her hair.

When Lewis Russell was trying to put one of his prize gamecocks back into the cage, it accidentally spurred him and got away. The only sure safe way of catching a runaway gamecock is to tire him out by teasing him with a hen. That's what he is doing in this picture. The gamecock kept lunging after the female and when he tired out, Lewis grabbed him by the feet and put him back in the pen.

BARN, SAGINAW, MICHIGAN

I saw the farmer feeding his sheep and I thought,
what a nice piece of rural America. We set the camera
up on the roadside and took this shot. Then the farmer
pointed out that the sheep near the truck had been
attacked by a wolf the previous night. That is reality
in rural America.

HALF DOME, YOSEMITE NATIONAL PARK, CALIFORNIA

If I were a painter, I would paint this area of Yosemite National Park. Half Dome comes as close to perfection in nature as any place I have ever visited. There is something haunting about the tension between the meadows of soft snow and the strong, chiseled mountain ranges. Shooting Half Dome is like photographing a beautiful woman; there simply are no bad angles. I have seen, perhaps, a thousand photographs of El Capitan and Half Dome and none of them is exactly alike. The weather plays a big role in shaping the mood of these powerful landscapes. On this occasion, I was shooting on a foggy day. I wanted a photograph that would capture the feel of sheer granite faces veiled by a silky mist.

VERNAL FALLS, YOSEMITE NATIONAL PARK, CALIFORNIA

Yosemite National Park is one of photography's "greatest hits." In other words, Yosemite is just awesome, and I rarely use that word to describe anything. While most of the shots I've taken here are from designated viewpoints, some have required considerable treks. Kelly Junkermann, a photographer friend of mine, carried the 4x5 camera for almost three miles into the Yosemite wilderness so I could get this shot, and the last mile was straight up a forty-degree grade, or at least it seemed like that. Someone in the group kept saying, "I remember this waterfall, it's just around the corner." Of course, the corner was two hours away.

The LeConte Memorial is a stately, churchlike structure nestled in a cluster of pines at the foot of a large mountain. The formal masonry building seemed out of character with its wild surroundings. Joseph LeConte was one of the first men who laid down the roads and established Yosemite as a national park. After spending enough time in the rugged backcountry of Yosemite, you develop a healthy respect for men like LeConte who explored this region without any of the conveniences. He deserved a memorial.

Depending on the quality of light and the length of
the exposure, a photograph of water in motion can look
like cotton candy, soapsuds, angel hair, a cloud formation, or meringue. In some ways, a still photograph
that is made from a long exposure of rushing water is
like a short movie, collapsed into a single frame. It
presents an infinitely variable drama that traces the
passage of water.

DESOTO FALLS, GEORGIA

I walked about two miles to shoot this picture of DeSoto Falls. No matter what part of this forest you explore, there is something special about walking into these backwoods. It is possible to feel that you are the first person that has ever been here, especially on an autumn day when the wind blows through dead leaves and cascading water rushes over the stones.

There are tree branches and roots here that you can walk on and climb. The way they are exposed forms an interesting network.

Upstate New York is one of the most beautiful parts of the country, and one of the coldest. I remember this shot very well because I actually missed the photograph I had stopped to take. Several minutes before this picture, sunlight was pouring through a small slit in the clouds, streaking the field with light. I set up the 4x5 as quickly as possible, hoping I could capture this on film. Unfortunately, I was too late. That critical moment of light was gone, but my camera was already in position on the tripod, so I waited, hoping the sun might peek through the clouds again. Standing in below-zero weather, however, I became discouraged and lost my patience. My hands had gone numb and the camera kept fogging over. So I packed the 4x5 and started to drive off. I didn't get very far. I glanced in the rearview mirror and stopped the car. There was something irresistible about this farmhouse, the gentle slope of the field, and the horse eating from its trough. So I backed up the car, took out my 35mm camera, and photographed this slice of rural America.

As I was driving from Rockford, Illinois, to La Crosse, Wisconsin, I spotted this little white church from the road. It was sitting in a glen surrounded by a stand of beautiful green trees. There is something about white wooden churches that touches me very deeply. It goes back to my childhood, when I remember sitting through services in a chapel that probably couldn't seat more than forty people. This is the kind of church where my grandmother and grandfather were buried. It has the real spirit of Americana that has been lost by many contemporary houses of worship. What I really liked here was the sense that it was the people who were in charge of this church, rather than the other way around.

One of the most spectacular drives in America, the twelve-mile loop through Red Rock Canyon is a photographer's dream. This stretch of road gave me the opportunity to shoot photographs that looked as if they could have been taken a hundred years ago, before civilization marred the natural landscape with telephone poles, high-tension wires, and the rusting skeletons of abandoned cars.

SAND DUNE, BEATTY, NEVADA

In one part of the valley, known as The Beehives, the forces of wind and water have shaped the rocks into mounds that could just as easily pass for giant shells left on the beach after a clambake. Just beyond this spot, the canyon opens up into Rainbow Vista, a mighty crest of red-orange sandstone, where the bands of striations bend like trees in the wind.

LINCOLN MEMORIAL, WASHINGTON, D.C.

Some sights, no matter how often you see them reproduced in photographs, have an extraordinary capacity to move you. For me the Lincoln Memorial is that kind of place. This photograph was taken at 2:00 A.M. I was absolutely amazed that there were probably thirty people there at that time of the morning.

There is something magnetic about the sculpture of Abraham Lincoln. His serene expression, with its unmistakable touch of tragedy around the eyes, draws people from all ages and walks of life, filling them with a new sense of dedication. With its stark simplicity and quiet grandeur, the Lincoln Memorial speaks of history and human aspirations, of the past, the present, and the future of America.